T0195024

VIBE HIGHER

SERENA JAMES

BALBOA.PRESS

A DIVISION OF HAY HOUSE

Balboa Press books may be ordered through booksellers or by contacting:

Balboa Press
A Division of Hay House
1663 Liberty Drive
Bloomington, IN 47403
www.balboapress.com
1 (877) 407-4847

Because of the dynamic nature of the Internet, any web addresses or links contained in this book may have changed since publication and may no longer be valid. The views expressed in this work are solely those of the author and do not necessarily reflect the views of the publisher, and the publisher hereby disclaims any responsibility for them.

The author of this book does not dispense medical advice or prescribe the use of any technique as a form of treatment for physical, emotional, or medical problems without the advice of a physician, either directly or indirectly. The intent of the author is only to offer information of a general nature to help you in your quest for emotional and spiritual well-being. In the event you use any of the information in this book for yourself, which is your constitutional right, the author and the publisher assume no responsibility for your actions.

Any people depicted in stock imagery provided by Getty Images are models, and such images are being used for illustrative purposes only. Certain stock imagery © Getty Images.

Print information available on the last page.

ISBN: 978-1-9822-3831-5 (sc)
ISBN: 978-1-9822-3833-9 (hc)
ISBN: 978-1-9822-3832-2 (e)

Library of Congress Control Number: 2019918070

Balboa Press rev. date: 11/30/2019

Contents

Introduction

"Does the walker choose the path, or the path the walker?"
-Garth Nix

There was a time when I wasn't aware of energy and the vital role it plays in our lives, but when I was first introduced to the concept it made complete sense to me. I had started using essential oils for their emotional and physical benefits. The suggested uses of a couple blends I had chosen recommended applying to the solar plexus and over the liver. Solar plexus? Of course I had to Google what a solar plexus was. I learned it is a chakra, a main energy center of the body, associated with balance, personal power, and individuality.

When the solar plexus chakra is not balanced, people can experience things like the need to control, aggression, or low self-esteem to name a few. The liver is known to store and process the emotion of anger. The very reason I was using these essential oil blends was to help with anger and aggression issues. After learning this, it made complete sense to apply the blends to the solar plexus and liver locations of the body. My exposure to the concept of energy would continue.

A friend referred me to an energy healer. I honestly hadn't really heard of energy healers before the referral, but I was up for anything and made an appointment. During the first appointment, the healer told me the anger was stuck in the stomach, the worst possible place, and should be flowing through the liver. I had already heard this before because of the essential oils. All the pieces were coming together. It seemed completely logical to me that if anger was in the stomach, but was supposed to be in the liver, that would likely cause some issues.

The energy healer released the anger from the stomach and cleared the energetic blockages so the anger could be properly processed by the liver. It would be just a couple of weeks when I would notice years of anger and aggression subside. It was mind-blowing and amazing. I immediately felt drawn to the work of an energy healer. I wondered why everyone wasn't talking about the power of energy healing.

As time went on, my energy healer let me know of an upcoming class where I would be able to learn energy healing techniques for myself. I didn't feel the timing was right with projects I had going at work, but she insisted it would be very helpful if I knew how to do these things for myself and my family. I realized that by me learning to do this, my healer would potentially be losing a client. If she was OK with that, I felt this was something I definitely needed to do.

The first training I attended was for a pendulum dowsing program called *Trailblazing Communications*. It was incredible. I quickly discovered with energy the possibilities were endless. After the training, I was required to complete 50 sessions on others before I would be certified. I had never felt more excited about "work" in my life and completed sessions for many people as quickly as possible.

It felt incredible helping others in this manner. The things that would come up for them, how accurate they were, and that I could actually help someone overcome obstacles in their lives was fascinating and fulfilling. I continued providing energy healing sessions long after my requirement for certification.

As time went on, I would learn other energy healing modalities as I felt called to do so: Reiki, The Pure Truth, and Access Bars. Having the ability to support myself, my family, and others based on all our unique needs was rewarding and empowering. My heart continued to be filled with this work, and my circle of healer friends was growing.

I would attend spiritual and healing gatherings as much as possible. I loved learning about people's abilities and divine gifts and connecting with others doing similar work. On several occasions people told me Archangel Jophiel was in my presence and that my guides wanted me to know I was on the right path. These messages would come to me in other ways as well.

I began seeing numerical patterns repeatedly, especially 911. I recall telling my life partner how often I was seeing this number all the time. He said I see lots of numbers, but this one was significant in society, so I recognized it. I didn't believe it was as simple as that, but I thought it meant something was wrong since 911 is known as an emergency number in the United States. I believe this was when I discovered angel numbers.

I looked up "meaning of 911". What I found was 911 is an angel number that encourages you to follow your divine life path. More signs came into my life pointing me in the direction of energy healing. I would soon find myself in a position to choose between my day job and my calling in life: I chose energy healing.

I couldn't wait to continue helping people when I finally honored my role in this world as an energy healer. It had always been difficult for me to watch people suffer and struggle, and I had finally embraced my divine gifts to support others and myself through energy healing. I started my own business offering one-on-one appointments and classes, but eventually more messages would come to me indicating I needed to do something more.

As I performed healing work on myself, a message would continually pop up that I was aiming too low. What could that mean? I had left a cozy job at a university to share my gifts with the world. I support many people with those gifts. I share love and light on social media and in my blog. And I'm working really hard! How could I be aiming too low?

Taking seriously this persistent message, I raised the stakes and set an intention to help millions of people all over the world feel their best. Yes, *millions*. If that isn't aiming high, I don't know what it is! However, the message of "aiming too low" still came to me.

I finally realized that to support millions of people, I would need to go further than individual appointments and the small-scale events I had been doing. That would be *a lot* of appointments and events, right? I had to go bigger. That's when the idea of a book first entered my mind.

Books can go everywhere. They can be read, shared, and downloaded and are accessible to more people than I could even see by appointment in a single lifetime. I needed to make a book happen. Finally, the message of "aiming too low" had ceased, confirming I was on the right track.

My book would have to be powerful. It would have to include healing energy within the pages. It would need to resonate with the reader. It would have actual steps and actions included that one could take right away to help them feel better than they did before that moment. It would provide real, noticeable benefits to anyone who read it.

With all that in mind, choosing a topic for this book was easy. I work with energy every single day but understand that most people aren't thinking about it like I do. Considering my goals for the readers of the book, talking about energy was an obvious choice. That's how *Vibe Higher* was born.

When you vibe higher you feel empowered and in control. You look forward to the possibilities each day has to offer. You understand you have amazing gifts to share with yourself and the world. You know that it's possible to reach your potential and go even further. You know you can overcome any challenge that crosses your path. Vibing higher undoubtedly increases your satisfaction with your human experience. It creates endless opportunities for awesomeness in your life.

To benefit from this book, it doesn't matter how much you know about energy or whether you're in a difficult situation or life is smooth sailing for you. *Vibe Higher* was created for everyone seeking tried and true ways to empower themselves and take control of how they show up in the world. It is for everyone choosing to experience all they desire.

As you read this book, you'll learn about energy, how it affects you, and how to care for it. You'll increase your self-awareness and can choose to absorb the loving, high vibrating energy stored within each page. Anytime your mind, body, and spirit need a boost, revisit your favorite sections of this book to raise your vibration. *Vibe Higher* is always here for you.

I am grateful you are here. I am excited for all the amazing possibilities coming your way.

What is Energy?

"Everything is energy and that's all there is to it."
-Darryl Anka

Energy is all around us and directly impacts how we feel and what we experience. Energy can help us or hinder us. It can propel us forward on our path or create difficulties. Either way, it's just energy, and we have the power to take control of our own vibrations. I intentionally stay away from saying "good" or "bad" energy, because energy is just energy and we can change it to meet our needs. Additionally, what's good or bad for one thing isn't necessarily good or bad for something else. As such, I classify energy in two ways: beneficial to us and non-beneficial to us.

Beneficial energy is what raises and maintains our healthy vibrations. Non-beneficial energy is what lowers our vibrations. Beneficial and non-beneficial energy can be felt and acquired from anywhere. Everything we consume and encounter physically, emotionally, and spiritually has the potential to affect our energy.

Ever walk into a room and all the sudden feel gross or uneasy, or you walk into a room and feel like you're right where you belong? That is energy. You feel these things because of how your energy reacts to the energy of that room and the people and objects in it.

Could you really have a lucky shirt that makes you have days where everything seems to go right? Yes! Could your dining room table be holding non-beneficial energy that causes your family to argue? Yes! Could you hold a seemingly harmless belief that actually keeps you from realizing the success you desire? Yes! Do I have first-hand experience with all this and more? Yes!

All of us have an energetic field that vibrates at a frequency. Everything has an ideal frequency, and when we are not vibrating at or above that frequency, we experience issues with our minds, bodies, and/or spirits. Everything has the potential to affect our energy in what we would interpret as a positive or negative effect. It is helpful to understand the sources of the energy affecting you so you can make decisions or take actions to protect and improve your personal energy. Let's discuss some of the many things that affect your energy.

People and Places

Interacting with other people and environments affects our energy. Have you ever felt drawn to certain people or places or nature? That's because their energy aligns with or enhances your energy. Conversely, some people and environments could be a turn off for you. This can happen for a couple of reasons. One, their vibration is much lower than yours and it makes you uncomfortable, or two, your vibration is much lower than theirs and it makes you uncomfortable. People we surround ourselves with can uplift us and can drain us. Places we go can energize us or deplete us. Now is a good time to mention energy vampires.

Energy vampire is a term used to describe people or places that drain our energy. They suck your energy for their own benefit without replacing it with beneficial energy. There is a big difference between empathizing with a loved one and having someone take your energy. You will be able to recognize that someone or some place is an energy vampire when each interaction you have with them seems to metaphorically suck the life out of you. You will feel depleted, drained, and possibly confused. You might even be contemplating at this moment who or where in your life might be an energy vampire. It could already be obvious as you consciously try to avoid certain people or places that you know don't make you feel good. But sometimes these people and places are unavoidable. In the *Vibe Higher: Protection* section later on this book, you will learn how to protect yourself.

Objects

Objects can affect our energy. It might seem difficult to acknowledge a table or a t-shirt could hold energy that affects us positively or negatively, but it is true. I have gotten rid of clothes and hand-me-down items for that very reason.

Sometimes these things simply need an energy clearing instead of tossed altogether, but it's important to recognize that simple objects that we put in our spaces or on our bodies can influence us. Things we keep in our homes and offices can motivate us or make us unproductive.

Antiques, yard sales, and buying used goods are popular methods for outfitting our homes and fulfilling our needs. It is imperative you understand items that have been in possession of others has the potential to carry their energy. When you invite it into your home, you also are accepting that energy, beneficial or non-beneficial. I mostly try to avoid buying used items because of this, but sometimes it is necessary. If you have items in your space you feel concerned about, follow the instructions in the upcoming *Vibe Higher: Object Cleansing* chapter.

Past Lives

Past life experiences can greatly impact what we experience now. I have read accounts of people experiencing pain in a specific area on their body and learning it was related to an injury from a past life. Trauma, emotions, beliefs, agreements, and oaths can also carry forward into this lifetime and are often related to obstacles we face. Non-beneficial past life energy can often be cleared through meditation or support with a holistic healer.

Ancestral and Generational Energy

Ancestral and generational energy affects us. Medical professionals use family history to assess a patient's risk

4

of developing disease and illness, so it's not a stretch to recognize that energetic patterns could be inherited. Not only can disease be passed on from previous generations, so can beliefs, attitudes, and curses. As with past life energy, ancestral and generational energy can be addressed during meditation or with guidance of a holistic healer.

Consumption

What we consume from what we eat and drink or what we read and watch affects our energy. Choosing foods and information that nourish us is advised, and we need to be discerning of what we consume. What we consume can drain us or energize us, make us feel well or unwell, or trigger positive or negative emotions. Be selective.

Thoughts

Our thoughts are energy. What we focus on is typically what we see. I once dated a man who had a very ugly pair of black jeans he liked to wear. Whenever we would go out on a date, I would think to myself over and over again, *I hope he doesn't wear those black jeans.* And every time he would show up in the black jeans. Did my focus on these black jeans manifest itself into reality? I believe so! You see, around this time I had discovered *The Secret* on Netflix, which is all about the Law of Attraction. I consciously shifted my focus from *please don't wear the black jeans* to *please wear more attractive pants*, and I kid you not, it worked. In any situation, focus on what you would like to experience, not what you don't. Our thoughts have the power to actualize into our reality.

Beliefs

Our beliefs are energy. As Louise Hay wisely states, "It is true if you believe it to be true." It doesn't matter if what you believe is actually true or not because it will be true for you. Think about an area of your life that could use some improvement, like money, weight, or relationships. Can you identify any beliefs that could be blocking you from feeling satisfied in those areas? Beliefs are common barriers holding people back from enjoying their life as they truly desire. Think about areas of your life you do feel satisfied with. What are your beliefs around those? Can you see the difference between beliefs supporting or hindering your reality? Our beliefs can help us realize success or keep us from realizing our full potential.

Non-beneficial beliefs can be more challenging to change versus non-beneficial thoughts. Not to mention that many of your beliefs may in fact not even be your own. Beliefs are formed by our experiences or programmed into our being by culture, family, media, environment, and past lives. They are deeply rooted energetically and can't be as easily manipulated as thoughts can. Need an example? Just look at unbudging beliefs within United States political parties! Vibing higher can help dissolve non-beneficial beliefs, and some holistic healers can tap into and clear beliefs that are no longer serving you in a positive capacity.

Energy is Everything

Some of this energy we can see and experience in the physical realm, and some we can't. It's all energy and we have the power to take control and break old, worn-out patterns to experience more of what we desire. It is our responsibility to care for ourselves and maintain a healthy vibration. Know that you have the power to improve your energy and your experiences.

Why Vibe Higher?

"Vibe high and the magic around you will unfold."
-Akilnathan Logeswaran

Good vibes. Positive energy. Vibe higher. What does that really mean? In pop culture, it refers to feeling good, spreading kindness, or doing your best. From a metaphysical standpoint, it literally means increasing your energetic vibration.

Your vibration is a major factor in how you feel and what you experience on an emotional, physical, and spiritual level. Simply put, if you'd like to feel better in any of those areas, raise your vibration. As you continue reading the following chapters, you will learn an important fundamental component of energy called frequency and various ways to increase your vibration.

Signs You're Vibing High

- Things come easy for you- relationships, work, money, love, things you desire.
- You realize success in your personal and professional life.
- You have minimal stress and feel clear-headed.
- You feel healthy on an emotional, physical, and spiritual level.
- You feel energized and rested.
- You make healthy choices for yourself.
- You attract desirable people and opportunities into your life.

Signs You're Vibing Low

- You feel disconnected.
- Your mind is foggy.
- You have little desire to do anything.
- You have an addiction (behaviors, substances, thoughts).
- You feel tired and stressed.
- You have frequent conflict at home, work, and/or school.
- You're in pain or feel unhealthy physically, emotionally, or spiritually.

As you look at the signs, recognize where you fit in. You might find some apply and some do not. You might also recognize yourself in both the high and low categories. These signs are only intended to raise your self-awareness, to give you a gauge of where you can focus your efforts. Something I have come to learn is oftentimes we get so used to our "normal" that we don't even realize we could have better. The key to your self-awareness is knowing your vibes. No matter what signs you see in yourself, my desire for you is to embrace the love, hope, and support offered to you within these pages.

Your energy not only affects you, but everyone and everything else you encounter. If you are a parent/caregiver or in a relationship, it is so important to know that your energy affects your loved ones even more so than others passing by. Taking care of yourself and your energy is one of the ultimate ways to show your love and commitment to the most important people in your life. That includes you, too! Vibing higher helps you create a happier, healthier life for yourself and your loved ones.

It is still possible to run into obstacles and challenges even when you're high vibing. You will learn why this happens and realize that your increased vibration enhances your ability to overcome them. Vibing higher shares similarities with positive thinking and healthy mindsets. It's mostly true that no one can be positive all the time, but embracing positivity while honoring true feelings supports people through difficult times. Likewise, vibing higher does not mean you'll never face challenges, but you understand your magic increases with your vibration.

High vibes. Low vibes. Your vibes. Their vibes. It's all energy. Some people are much more sensitive to energy than others. They can even take on energy that isn't theirs. They are called empaths. Let's explore what it means to be an empath in the next chapter.

Are You an Empath?

"Derived from the Greek word 'em' (in) and 'pathos'
(feeling), the term 'empath' refers to a person who
is able to 'feel into' the feelings of others."
-Mateo Sol

It is beautiful and quite a gift to be an empath, but it can be difficult to navigate as well. Empaths are feelers and highly intuitive. This means empaths are naturally tuned into energy without even trying. Empaths are often helpers, a shoulder to lean on, and feel connected with nature. When aware of their abilities, empaths can transmute energy into something more helpful and beneficial.

Are you an empath? There are several considerations to help you decide. You might be an empath if:

- you feel overwhelmed in crowds or out in public,
- you can easily detect how others around you are feeling,

- you have an awareness of the interconnectedness of all things in the Universe,
- you or others around you would describe you as sensitive,
- people, even random strangers, share their problems or life stories with you, and/or
- you have a working relationship with your intuition.

Empaths can feel everything and are susceptible to taking on the energy of what's around them. They might feel what they are experiencing as if it is their own thoughts or emotions when in fact it could belong to someone or something else. In extreme cases, empaths can also take on the behaviors and personalities of energies surrounding them. It is helpful for an empath to release this energy to care for their own well-being. If you are unsure if an emotion, physical feeling, or behavior belongs to you or someone/something else, you can use this statement:

Please release this energy that is not my own
and transmute it into something better.

If it did in fact belong to someone or something else, you will feel that emotion or physical feeling disappear within moments of reciting the clearing statement above. If it was yours, it will remain, and you can take steps to address it if necessary. If you have empathic abilities, it is important to protect yourself and your own energy.

Taking on energy can really be confusing and exhausting. For these reasons, an energetic filter is an appropriate way to protect yourself. You will still be able to recognize the energy of what is around you, but you won't take it on as if it was your own. To create an energetic filter, visualize a screen surrounding you and say:

This filter will discern what is mine and what is theirs and will prevent theirs from affecting me in a non-beneficial way.

You can set this intention yourself, but if you feel you need assistance, consult with a holistic healer to do it for you. Just like a literal filter, sometimes energetic filters need cleaning. When you feel yourself physically, emotionally, or spiritually taking on energy that does not belong to you, you know it is time to clean your filter. You can do so by repeating the statement from above or again working with your holistic healer.

If you are a parent or caregiver and suspect your child is an empath, it is very important to create a protective filter for them, especially if they attend school outside of the home. There are many types of energies at schools that can be too much to process for your empathic beacon of light. If your child is having behavior difficulties or heightened emotions, it is a strong possibility they are an empath. Understanding this as a possibility for your child will help you better support them to harness their gifts and feel their best.

Now that you understand how energy affects us and what it is to be an empath, it's time to talk about an important aspect of energy: frequency.

Frequency: The Key to Energy

"Energy cannot be created or destroyed, it can
only be changed from one form to another."
-Albert Einstein

Frequency is a measurement of energy. Everything is energy
and has a vibration measured by frequency. A popular way
to take this measurement is through pendulum dowsing.
With a pendulum and a dowsing chart, a pendulum dowser
can measure the frequency of anything. Seriously anything.
People, animals, emotions, thoughts, beliefs, objects, goals,
intentions, places, land, elements, food…everything! It all
has a frequency.

Frequency can help determine exactly where something
is vibrating energetically and if that frequency needs to be
increased or decreased to have more desirable experiences.
What comes to mind when you think of Albert Einstein?

Genius? Me, too. So when Albert Einstein tells us in the quote leading this chapter that energy can only change forms, we can embrace that concept and realize we have the power to shift our energy to benefit our well-being.

Ideal frequency is the vibration of any person, place, object, or thought where it experiences ultimate well-being. You have an ideal frequency as well as everything around you. At your ideal frequency you have the potential to feel your best and experience all the amazing things you desire like love, wellness, and abundance. When you are vibrating below your ideal frequency, it's possible to experience struggle, discomfort, or sickness in any area of your life.

When we're exposed to energy vibrating lower than our ideal frequency, that energy would be non-beneficial to us and has the potential to negatively impact our vibrations either temporarily or for an extended period of time. Low-vibrating energy affecting us that has not been neutralized or released has a tendency to stick around and can manifest itself into bigger issues later in life. When energy around us is vibrating at or higher than our ideal frequency, that is beneficial energy and has the potential to positively impact our vibrations immediately and in the long run. It is all energy, and it can affect you on every level. Because our energy fields are constantly exposed to both beneficial and non-beneficial energy, it is necessary to care for it like we care for other aspects of our wellness.

Even if you are not a pendulum dowser or are unable to measure frequency, just understanding the power of frequency is beneficial to you. This is where your thoughts, beliefs, and actions become very important. If your desire is to own your own business, find love, or be healthy, you must align your energy with the energy of these desires. Think like a business owner, a lover, a healthy person. Believe you are a business owner, a lover, a healthy person. Fully envision yourself experiencing your desires. Take actions and find opportunities to work toward your desires.

Now that you are understanding how energy affects you, it is important to remember to honor yourself. Recognize what you need and know it is not selfish to take care of yourself.

Are you ready to discover ways to take care of your energy? In the following chapters, you'll learn exactly how you can raise your vibration almost immediately. Some of the suggestions might be for you and some might not. It is totally your choice. You will discover which ones are your favorites and work best for you. You have the power to control your energy, now is the time to learn how to do so.

Vibe Higher: Affirmations

Affirmations are words of empowerment you can say to yourself or aloud. They can be used to transform your thoughts and beliefs into something more beneficial to your well-being. Repeating affirmations has the power to increase your vibration and align yourself with the frequency of the words you are absorbing.

You can write or record your own affirmations or find them in books and online. It is important your affirmations are validating and written in present tense or like you have already accomplished it. You should avoid writing affirmations with negative words. For example, *I will lose 10 pounds* would be an ineffective affirmation. A better affirmation would be, *I weigh a healthy 150 pounds*. Another example of a low-vibrating affirmation would be, *I will find my dream job*. It would be more powerful to say, *I work in my dream job*.

There are several ways to use and display your affirmations. You can write them yourself, type them, record your own voice memos, and say them aloud or to yourself. People will write them on their mirrors, say them aloud while looking at themselves in the mirror, record them on sticky notes and hang in high visibility places, or keep them in their wallets. It is completely your preference how you would like to use your affirmations. You can even experiment with different ways to find what works best for you. Remember repetition is key to the effectiveness of affirmations. Below you will find an exercise that will instantly raise your vibration.

Affirmation Exercise

This affirmation exercise can increase your vibration by up to 100%. You will need either a pen and paper, a computer word processing app, or a notes app on your phone.

Write "I am <<INSERT DESIRE>>" 25 times.

For example, *I am prosperous, I am healthy, I am love, I am worthy of...*, etc.

Reflect on how you feel after completing this exercise. You can repeat this exercise daily until you believe what you have written to be true. At that time, you can repeat the exercise with a new desire.

One of my favorite affirmations is *I am prosperous.* Prosperity embodies ultimate well-being for the mind, body, and spirit.

Vibe Higher: Alone Time

If you are someone who has difficulty finding time for just yourself, alone time is a way great to help you recharge. It is likely you are giving too much of yourself to everyone and everything, so it is important to have time to yourself not giving in to the demands of anyone or anything else. Remember, it is not selfish to take time for yourself. Just ten minutes of shutting yourself off from the world can be beneficial. Alone time can be spent doing something you love, spoiling yourself, meditating, or simply doing nothing at all. You get to choose! Just a note, Facebooking is not alone time! Shut off your phone, turn of the TV, and allow yourself to just be.

It can be a struggle to take time for yourself, so if you're a planner, put "Alone Time" in your calendar to have a moment in each week to just be with yourself, even if it is for only a few moments. And if you're not a planner, still put it in your calendar. Some people will wake up a half hour earlier each day to just focus on themselves. For me, I have an appointment with my massage therapist every single month.

Complete the following exercise to help you incorporate alone time into your schedule.

Alone Time Exercise

In this exercise, you will plan for alone time. Alone time can raise your vibration by up to 90%, so it is worth taking time to plan for it by answering the following questions.

- What activity or service will help you recharge?
- Does someone need to provide a service for you, or can you do it for yourself?
- Do you need alone time each day, week, or month?
- How much alone time can you fit into your schedule that will be beneficial to you?

Choose how you'll spend your alone time and add it to your calendar or reminders.

Vibe Higher: Aromatherapy

Aromatherapy is the use of essential oils to support the mind, body, and spirit. Essential oils are carefully extracted from plants through steam distillation, cold-pressing, and resin tapping and have been used for their many benefits for centuries. Their frequencies can elevate our frequency with the potential to increase our vibration by 100%. Energetic benefits can be experienced by using essential oils aromatically or topically with most people feeling a positive difference within minutes.

Essential oils are very potent and powerful, meaning one drop can go a long way. You can diffuse, use in a detox bath, or wear as a fragrance. To diffuse, add a few drops of your favorite essential oil in a cold-water diffuser. If you do not have a diffuser, you can add a few drops to a cotton ball and place in a vent, or simply add to the palms of your hands, rub together, and inhale. For a bath, you can combine your essential oils with Epsom or Himalayan salt. As a fragrance, you can apply to your wrists, back of neck, behind the ears, shoulders, or to chakras.

Essential oils with the highest frequencies include rose, helichrysum, frankincense, myrrh, and German chamomile. You can also mix together your favorite essential oils to create your own custom blend. Be sure to use high quality essential oils. With the growing popularity of the aromatherapy industry, many companies are cutting corners by adding synthetics and adulterants to their oils to increase yield and cut costs. Seek trusted brands that are reasonably priced and not overly inexpensive.

Detox Bath Recipe

Mix together 1/2 to 1 cup sea salt or Epsom salt with 2-3 drops of an essential oil of your choice and add to a warm bath. Try to soak for at least 20 minutes. Essential oils like Frankincense, Lavender, or Rose are recommended. Try to select gentle essential oils that won't feel hot or uncomfortable on your skin. Ensure the essential oil you choose is safe to be used topically by checking the label.

Vibe Higher: Breathing

We already know breathing is essential for life, but much of the time we don't even pay any attention to the rhythm of our breath as we go about our day. That's why focused breathing and breathing exercises can play an important role in our well-being. The benefits of focused breathing are numerous: reduced stress, increased clarity, grounding, and stabilizing. Many other activities like yoga, intense exercise, and meditation, recognize the power of tuning into your breath as a major component of successful results. That's because awareness and control over our breath is valuable.

Focusing on your breath and breathing methodically is helpful for raising your vibration. Breathing exercises can increase your frequency by up to 50% within a few minutes. These exercises can be completed as part of a daily routine or as needed. There are several different types of breathing exercises you can find online to practice or use the one below. Experimenting with different types of exercises will help you choose which ones work best for you.

Breathing Exercise

If possible, comfortably seat yourself with both feet planted on the floor. Inhale deeply through your nose, filling first your abdomen and then your chest. Hold that breath for a few seconds, then slowly exhale through the mouth.

Repeat until you can feel the stress and tension leaving your mind and body or up to six times in a row. You can incorporate this breathing exercise or another one of your choice into your daily self-care routine.

Vibe Higher: Crystals

Crystals have serious healing properties and can greatly assist you in improving your energy. Each type of crystal has a specific healing purpose, so you can select a crystal based on your physical, emotional, or spiritual needs. Using crystals has the potential to increase your vibration by up to 80%. When possible, it is recommended to select your crystals yourself, in-person, so you can choose ones that seem to "speak" to you.

You can meditate with your crystal, strategically place it somewhere in your home, office, or vehicle, or place it on your chakras. When meditating with crystals, you can hold them in your hands to absorb their energy. There are strategies for placing crystals in the home and office, but you can also hold your crystal and carry with you through different areas of the space and see where your crystal seems to pull itself towards to determine where to place it. When resting crystals on the body, keeping them there for about 20 minutes is most beneficial.

Before you use a crystal, you should cleanse it and set your intention of what you'd like to experience by using that crystal. Cleansing your crystals will release any type of non-beneficial energy your crystal may have absorbed and enhance its energetic properties. To cleanse your crystals, place it in either the light of a full moon or in sea salt overnight. Crystal cleansing should be done periodically. You will know it's time to cleanse your crystal when it feels like its abilities in supporting you are decreasing.

Popular crystals for dispelling negative energy and improving your vibration include smoky quartz, quartz, and black tourmaline.

Crystal Exercise

After you have selected a crystal, cleansed it, and set an intention for it, you are ready to use it. If possible, find a quiet space for a brief meditation. Seated in a meditative position or lying down, hold your crystal in both your hands. Close your eyes and breathe deeply in and out three times. Focus on the crystal and envision its energy flowing through your hands to throughout the rest of your body, with every cell of your body absorbing its energy. Feel the healing vibrations in each and every cell in your body. When the vibrations begin to quiet, slowly return to the present moment by gently moving your fingers and toes and opening your eyes. Take another deep breath in, slowly exhale, and say *thank you.*

Vibe Higher: Declutter

Clutter can wreak havoc on your energy. It takes up space both physically and energetically in a chaotic manner. Clutter is also problematic because it fills you with things you do not desire, leaving no room for the things you do desire. If you'd like to invite more positive experiences into your life, decluttering is a great place to begin. When you physically clear clutter, you are telling the Universe you have made space for something better and more beneficial in your life.

Being messy and having clutter are not the same thing. Messy is not putting things back in their places or cleaning up after yourself. Clutter is having things that you truly do not need. If you've lived somewhere for years, chances are you've built up a fair amount of clutter. With the many demands in our lives, it's easy to skip out on decluttering, but this action can greatly benefit you as it can increase your vibration by up to 85%.

Remember when we talked about objects holding energy? Our clutter can hold all kinds of energy, including non-beneficial energy, and yes, that energy affects you. I know that making it to this point in the book, you're getting really good at tuning into your energy. If you come across something that feels like it shouldn't be in your possession anymore, get rid of it. If you are having difficulty parting with something, keep it. Trust the vibes you're getting from each object.

Years ago, my mother cleared out the belongings of four of her family homes. I came to care for many of these items, which meant boxes and boxes of items stored in my home. It was so overwhelming I could never bring myself to deal with it, until I finally realized I didn't have to deal with it all at one time. If you're feeling overwhelmed by the clutter you've accumulated in your life, start small with a manageable project. You can set aside a certain amount of time you'll dedicate to decluttering, or you can begin with a specific box or room. Do not feel like you need to take care of it all at once. Whichever way you work best is the way to do it. There is no wrong way.

Decluttering Exercise

Locate a cluttered space calling your attention: a desk, your nightstand, the kitchen counter, or a room for example. Remove all items that do not belong there and put them in their appropriate spot. If you come across items you do not have use for, you can toss them, donate them, or see if someone else has a use for them. Repeat this exercise as often as you feel necessary.

Vibe Higher: Exercise

Being active is beneficial for the mind, body, and spirit. Exercise is known to boost clarity and positive feelings. Intense workouts like kickboxing or high-intensity interval training (HIIT) can be an incredible release of tense, stressful energy. Gentle workouts like yoga and walking can help clear your mind and make you feel more grounded. Playing a sport for fun or competition can be social and enjoyable. Find an exercise or workout you enjoy doing so you'll be more likely to do it.

I have never been a gym rat in my life, but several years ago I did a 10-week body challenge at a gym with a friend. Workouts were six times a week. I didn't lose much weight, however the physical results were visible as my body became stronger and more toned. But that wasn't the best part: I had never felt stronger, more focused, and clear-headed. Confidence in my abilities to parent, defend myself if needed, and to problem-solve skyrocketed. I know that committing to a time-intensive workout routine like a 10-week body challenge can be difficult, so finding a solution that will work for your schedule is most important.

Seek out classes in your community that interest you or find a workout partner to help keep each other accountable. Check out your local recreation department to see what kinds of league sports are available. If those ideas don't fit your schedule or budget, you can find tons of videos and workout plans online that you can do at home or at the office. Exercise can increase your vibration by up to 100% during and after your workout, and not to mention the long-term benefits you'll experience because of your efforts.

Exercise Goal Setting Activity

Get out a pen and paper and write an exercise goal for yourself. Include details like how many minutes of exercise you'd like to get per week, what type(s) of exercise you are willing to do, when you will make time to exercise, who do you need to help you, and where you will exercise. If you are doing exercises with repetitions (like jumping jacks, squats, push-ups, sit-ups, etc.), set a timer for one minute and see how many reps you can do of that exercise in that time to establish your baseline. Set a goal of increasing the number of reps by 10-20% over the next 30 days.

Vibe Higher: Food and Drink

How you nourish yourself impacts your vibration. Choose food and drink that is right for you. Notice I didn't say things like only eat fresh produce or ditch meat and fatty foods? That's because every individual body is different, and our nutritional needs vary. You might rarely consume meat, but occasionally feel your body craving a steak. You might not have a lot of sugar in your diet, but sometimes your brain needs a can of Coke to fuel up. Listen to your body. You will know what you eat and drink is right for you if you feel energized, joyous, and healthy when and after consuming it. If you feel drained, sluggish, or even sick after eating or drinking something, that's a strong signal you should avoid those foods and drinks.

Be cautious of dieting. There are a lot of fad diets out there that people gravitate to and can even experience wonderful results. However, once the dieting is finished, people go back to their old ways and even sometimes gain more weight than what they lost. Focus on *diet* (what you consume regularly) over *dieting* (making temporary diet changes to achieve a short-term goal). Your diet is part of your lifestyle and choosing the right food and drink for you will have a positive effect on your well-being.

Use the Food and Drink Exercise in this section to help you discover what you should keep or ditch from your diet. Please note, if you are doing a diet overhaul, you might experience discomfort in the beginning as your body adjusts to your new way of life. This is a common occurrence. Hang in there, know it will pass, and be proud of yourself for making better choices for your overall health and wellness.

Food and Drink Exercise

Find food and drinks that make you feel great by keeping a food journal. In your journal, record what you consume and how you feel. You can use a 10-point scale, with 1 being low and 10 being high, to indicate your energy level throughout the day. You can also assess your mood throughout the day (happy, fun, affectionate, sad, tired, angry, annoyed, etc.). You can keep this journal for as long as you'd like. Use your entries to help you determine a correlation between how you feel and what you've consumed to help you make better choices in the future.

Vibe Higher: Gratitude

Gratitude is very powerful for raising vibrations. Studies suggest that gratitude can even lower anxiety and depression. Practicing gratitude means actively feeling grateful or demonstrating acts of gratefulness. You can increase your vibration by up to 60% each time you practice gratitude.

You can have gratitude for anything: your gifts and abilities, people in your life, your successes and accomplishments, your material possessions, and your experiences and opportunities. Showing and expressing gratitude towards others, nature, and animals is also beneficial. Practicing gratitude might be one of the quickest ways to increase your vibration, you can do it anywhere, and it really doesn't require any special materials to do so. However, if you feel like nothing is really going right in your life, you might find it difficult to recognize things to be grateful for. There is a solution to support you.

Gratitude doesn't always have to be for something you already have or have experienced, it can be for something you desire. For example, you can be grateful for your promotion at work, your ability to pay bills with ease, for having strength and patience, or for finding an honest and loving life partner. Those are just some examples, but you can see that you can have gratitude for what you wish to experience. By giving thanks to something you desire, you are consciously aligning yourself with the frequency of that reality.

Practicing all this gratitude might have you wondering who exactly you are thanking. That's up to you. It could be yourself, your higher self, a higher power, spirit guides, the Universe, Mother Earth, or the very people receiving your gratitude. Any, some, or all will work. It is your choice.

Gratitude Exercises

The following are three different exercises. You can choose which ones work best for you.

- Say three things you are grateful for at this moment.
- Think about something you desire, but haven't yet actualized, and give it gratitude.
- At the beginning and ending of each day, focus on something you are grateful for, and say *thank you*.

Vibe Higher: Grounding and Nature

Grounding is the practice of reconnecting yourself with Mother Earth. It helps you feel more stabilized and secure. Our interconnectedness with nature is a fundamental component of our overall well-being. However, due to the stressful nature of everyday living, it is quite common for people to become ungrounded.

When people are ungrounded, they can feel out of control, frustrated, foggy, restless, disoriented, or out of balance. They will literally feel disconnected from *something*. That *something* might be unknown to the individual, but it is nature and Mother Earth they're feeling disconnected from.

Reconnecting with Mother Earth through grounding or being outdoors can increase your vibration by up to 100%. While being outdoors is beneficial in and of itself, consciously connecting with nature is even more powerful. That would include walking barefoot when safe to do so, inviting Nature Spirits into your mind and body, deeply breathing in fresh air, appreciating the beauty around you, or intuitively listening to Mother Earth. Sometimes location, weather, or mobility can limit your ability to physically get out in nature, but fortunately you can still ground yourself even indoors.

If you're a first-time grounder, it might be possible you will need to do it several times in the beginning, say once a day for a week. You will become in tune with your needs and understand how you feel when you are and are not grounded. Eventually you will be able to do "maintenance grounding", where you do it periodically when you know you need it.

Grounding Exercise

Plant your feet firmly on the ground, sitting or standing. You can be indoors or outdoors either barefoot or with shoes or socks. If you are unable to plant your feet on the ground or are indoors, envision that your feet are planted in lush, green grass. Close your eyes and imagine your feet turning into tree-like roots, growing longer and twisting through the floor or ground, to the earth, and going deeper and deeper. Feel the love and strength in your roots and your connection between yourself and Mother Earth. When you feel yourself stabilized and balance, you can carry on with your day.

Vibe Higher: Hobbies

Never underestimate the physical, emotional, and spiritual benefits of actively pursuing your interests. If there is something you really like to do that brings you peace and joy, make time to work on it. Hobbies allow you to be creative or adventurous and utilize your talents and gifts you might not always get to share and explore during a typical day. You can work on your hobbies alone or find other people and groups that share your interests.

Hobbies are typically leisure activities done outside of your regular work, but you might be someone who loves what you do as a career. Because you are often filled with joy through your vocation, you might not think you have time or a need for a hobby. However, exploring interests outside of your day-to-day can still be greatly beneficial to you. Enjoying a healthy hobby can help increase your vibration by up to 80%.

If you already have a hobby, think about how often you make time for this hobby. Is it enough for you? If you don't already have a hobby, answer the questions in the Hobby Exercise to generate ideas.

Hobby Exercise

What do you like to do for fun?

What is something you'd like to learn more about?

What is something you've always wanted to try, but haven't?

What is something you're good at, but don't ever really get to do?

What kinds of groups or organizations are available in your community? Do any pique your interest?

Vibe Higher: Laughing

Laughter is the best medicine as the saying goes. There is some truth to that. Laughing has the power to increase your vibration by 100% within seconds. Laughter is now being incorporated into wellness activities, like yoga and therapy, because it is so beneficial. Stress relieving and high vibrating, laughter is a great way to boost your energy.

Laughing is honestly one of my favorites. My life partner is a riot and has me in tears from laughter almost every single day. Among the many things I adore about him, his ability to make me laugh is one of my favorites.

You don't actually have to think something is amusing to use laughter to raise your vibration. Have you ever witnessed someone fake laugh and then get such a kick out of their fake laugh they begin laughing for real? There is no doubt laughter can be an instant mood booster.

Laughter Exercise

Look into a mirror or the camera on your phone, whichever is available to you. First begin by smiling at yourself. Then begin to laugh, mouth open, exaggerated laughing. Let the laughter fill your belly. Allow the tones and rhythms of your chuckles to vary. Embrace the uniqueness and variety in the sounds of your laughter. Continue with this practice for 3 minutes, or until you are actually laughing and ready to quit.

Vibe Higher: Media

Media is mass communications, from printed publications to audio/visual broadcasts, to experiences on the Internet. All forms of media are trying to reach you with their messaging. Media is always trying to tell you what to think, how to feel, what to buy, and what to believe through advertising and information output.

Studies and anecdotal information suggest humans are more interested in "bad news" than "good news". From a marketing perspective, negative news generates more engagement than feel-good stories. The impact this has on a consumer is a constant feed of information intended to disturb, anger, and force an opinion. While it is not a bad thing to raise awareness for issues that could use improvement, media tends to sensationalize or biasedly skew information to sell a better story than their competitors.

In addition to negative news, there is also a lot of entertainment media that essentially adds no value to your life, but takes up time and potentially other resources.

There is nothing wrong with watching TV or movies or scrolling through the Internet, but it can be problematic if it becomes excessive. Binging TV shows regularly or spending majority of your time on your phone can negatively impact your physical, emotional, and spiritual well-being. As with anything, finding balance is key.

Media is the ultimate mind-programmer, which can be either beneficial or non-beneficial. Be careful what you consume visually and aurally. There is a lot of useless information trying to take up valuable space in your mind. Media has the power to equally decrease or increase your vibration by 100% depending on what you're consuming. Be discerning. Feed your mind with healthy, helpful content that makes you feel good and adds value to your life.

Media Exercise

Increase your awareness of what you're consuming. First, roughly estimate how often you are interacting with media. That includes browsing the Internet, watching television, listening to the radio, etc. After reading or watching something, assess your mood and thoughts, and question the value it added to (or decreased from) your well-being. Finally, determine if your media consumption habits could be improved.

Vibe Higher: Object Cleanse

Remember in the beginning of this book we talked about how objects can affect our energy? I had mentioned how antiques and used items should be approached with caution. Anytime you acquire used items, they should be cleansed energetically. If you have an object in any of your spaces that you feel concerned about, be sure to use the Cleansing Prayer in this section to help you. You can also use this Cleansing Prayer for any new items you bring into your space as you feel necessary. To perform the cleansing prayer, either think of or physically be in the vicinity of the object.

Cleansing Prayer

This two-step Cleansing Prayer can be used on any object in your possession.

Step 1 – As you envision the non-beneficial energy dissipating, recite this prayer three times:

Please release all non-beneficial energy affecting this object.

Step 2 – After completing Step 1, recite this prayer three times:

> *Please fill the void with the most appropriate and beneficial energy in the past, present, and future as it affects the mind, body, and spirit on all levels.*

Vibe Higher: Prayer and Meditation

Whether it's only a couple minutes or for an extended period of time, prayer and meditation are very grounding and can increase your vibration by up to 70%. Prayer and meditation spiritually connect you with Source, Mother Earth, spiritual beings, or your higher self.

There is no formula for how often you should pray or meditate. Some people designate a specific time each day, others do it throughout the day, and some only do it on occasion as they feel necessary. If you've never prayed or meditated before, you might feel intimidated or unsure how to go about it. The thing about praying and meditating is there is no wrong way to do it. With either, you can focus your experience on expressing gratitude, asking for support and guidance, sharing your worries or successes, or just simply taking a moment to regroup and regain focus.

When praying you can talk with Source, spiritual helpers,

or your higher self just like you would with a close friend or family member. There are also many options for meditating: guided or self-led, silent or music or nature sounds, brief or deep, experiential, walking, and so on. You can explore various methods of meditation to find which ones you prefer.

The Guided Meditation Exercise in this section will bring feelings of peace and relaxation.

Guided Meditation Exercise

Find a quiet and safe space for this meditation exercise. Do not perform this meditation while operating a vehicle. You may find it helpful to record your voice reading the meditation prompts, then playing it back to yourself to fully engage in the experience.

Begin your meditation practice by closing your eyes.

Sit comfortably with a straight spine or lying down, whichever you prefer.

Place your hands on your legs or at your sides with palms facing up.

Take a deep breath in.

Slowly breathe out.

Breathe in peace and calm.

Breathe out stress and tension.

Notice your breath.

When you breathe in, let it fill your belly, your ribs, your chest, and your throat.

Hold at the top of your breath for a moment.

Breathe out.

Breathe in peace and calm.

Breathe out stress and tension.

Focus your attention on your breath and being present in this moment.

If your mind wanders, acknowledge the thought and let it go.

Then bring yourself back to this moment by focusing on your breath.

Visualize yourself walking in nature.

Some place calming.

Some place peaceful.

Some place where you feel relaxed and comforted.

Look around you.

What colors do you see?

What sounds do you hear?

Take it all in and enjoy the moment.

Hear the calming sounds of rushing water.

Follow the sound, continuing on your path.

The sound is getting louder.

You can smell the fresh water as you get closer and closer to the source.

Keep walking.

You can see it now.

A waterfall at the end of your path.

Go to the waterfall and run your hands through the gentle falling waters.

Now fully experience the waterfall by standing underneath it.

Feel the pure water gently cleanse you from any energy you no longer need.

Embrace this moment as the waterfall washes away anything blocking you from experiencing all that you desire.

The gentle, cleansing waters purify your aura.

Take a moment to enjoy the love and freedom these waters are gifting you.

The energy no longer serving you has now been released.

You step out of the waterfall and begin your journey back toward home.

The warmth of the sun dries you and energizes you.

As you follow the path back home, smile that you now have space for the things you truly desire.

You feel safe.

You feel secure.

You feel comforted.

You feel free.

Bring your attention back to your breath.

Breathe in peace and calm.

Slowly exhale.

Breathe in love and light.

Slowly exhale.

Before you open your eyes, begin to awaken your body with gentle neck stretches.

Breathe in.

As you exhale, lower your right ear towards your right shoulder.

Breathe in as you return to center.

Exhale, leaning your left ear towards your left shoulder.

Breathe in and return to center.

Return to your regular breath.

Wiggle your fingers.

Now gently massage your ears with your thumb and fingers. Massage your ear lobes and the rims of your ears.

Relax. You may stay in this moment as long as you like, opening your eyes when you are ready.

When you open your eyes, you will feel refreshed and recharged.

Vibe Higher: Protection

Protecting yourself doesn't necessarily raise your vibration immediately, but it is so important to help you maintain a healthy vibration. As you already know, our energetic fields are constantly interacting with other energetic fields. Some of that energy is beneficial and some is non-beneficial. The exercise in this section is simple, yet effective, for protecting your energy. Protecting yourself is essential to feeling your best. It is much more difficult for low vibrating energies, such as energy vampires, to affect you when you consciously protect your energy.

Protection Exercise

Envision an energetic bubble around you. Set the intention this bubble protects you from non-beneficial energy and lets in only the most beneficial energy.

Repeat this exercise anytime you feel your energetic boundaries have weakened.

Vibe Higher: Rest

Adequate rest is effective to help you maintain a healthy vibration. Taking a quick snooze when your mind needs a break can boost your vibration by up to 85%. Rest is so beneficial that even companies across the world provide space and time for employees to take power naps. Being rested can help improve mood, increase creativity and productivity, and enhance overall wellness.

All of us have different needs when it comes to rest. Forget the whole "8 hours a night" myth. Learn how much sleep is best for you and try to get that much sleep. You will know you are getting enough rest when you feel mostly energized throughout your day. If your career requires extensive mental stamina, you might find much benefit from the occasional power nap. Power naps can be as short as 5 minutes but should not exceed 15 minutes. The bottom line is when you need rest, rest as it is safe and permitted to do so.

Rest isn't always about bedtime or naps either. So many of us load up our schedules for every day of the week and it can be so exhausting. A full day of rest every once in awhile can be extremely beneficial. A day of rest means taking a break from the rushed and overloaded lifestyle trap we so often fall into. It alleviates the pressure of finishing house projects, working overtime, and obligating ourselves to be places we don't really need to be. It's OK to have a lazy day here and there to help you recover from overwork and hectic scheduling.

Sleep Quality Exercise

Many people struggle with getting quality sleep. If that applies to you, there are several natural things you can try to help you get better sleep:

- Establish a bedtime routine, trying to get to bed around the same time each day or night. If you already have a routine, try changing the time you normally go to bed.
- Try different sleepwear.
- Switch out your bedding if possible.
- Add a weighted blanket over your bedding.
- Avoid eating at least two hours before bedtime.
- Avoid electronics at least 30 minutes before bedtime.
- Diffuse or apply essential oils to the bottoms of your feet and back of neck. Essential oils helpful for sleep include Cedarwood, Lavender, Roman Chamomile, and Vetiver.
- Read a physical book.

Vibe Higher: Social Time

Whether it is time with family or friends, remember the value of socializing with others that make you feel vibrant. It is so easy to neglect social time when trying to fulfill daily obligations, but being in the company of people who raise your vibration is healthy for your mind, body, and spirit.

I remember when my parents first started heading south for the winter. Many of their friends also did the same. I quickly realized they spent more time with their friends when they were away from home. That might seem odd until you recognize when we are "home", we are typically busy taking care of today, catching up from yesterday, and planning for tomorrow. Human connection is necessary and one of the most things to conveniently neglect.

I also fondly recall spending time with my grandma and being invited out to one of her girlfriend's for pie. Her friend had out the fancy plates and coffee cups in which she served fresh pie and coffee as we girls gabbed and enjoyed each other's company. It was a wonderful time! And I don't believe since I've been invited to anyone else's home, or I've invited anyone to my home, for afternoon dessert and good company. Our efforts to connect face-to-face are decreasing in our digital age, but the vibrational benefits are not.

Social media does not replace actual social time. In fact, social media is almost the opposite of social. Yes, you can comment and interact with others, but the practice and importance of human connection diminishes as we sit behind our screens. Even talking on the phone is more engaging and higher vibrating than social media interactions and texting. It is up to us to reclaim the practice of genuine human interaction.

It doesn't matter if social time is for 15 minutes or an entire afternoon or evening, it is still beneficial. It doesn't matter if social time is calling up a good friend on the phone or going out to do something fun together, it is still beneficial. Social time has the power to increase your vibration by up to 100%. It does take effort to plan for and organize social time, but it is so worth it.

Social Time Exercise

The following exercises are practical suggestions to help you get more social time in your life.

- Invite a friend or acquaintance out to coffee.
- Invite friends over for dinner.
- Plan a "date night" with a good friend who doesn't live in the same community as you to catch up over the phone.
- Invite friends to join you at a community event.

Vibe Higher: Smile

Say cheese! The act of smiling can increase your vibration by up to 40%. Even smiling when you don't feel like smiling has a positive effect on your vibration as it signals your brain that you are happy, promoting feelings of joy and ease.

It is possible that smiling might not be representative of your current emotional state making it more difficult to do so. Vibing higher allows you to feel authentically and process through your emotions so you can move on when you are ready. You might not feel like smiling at those times, but when you are ready, smiling will help boost your mood and energy level.

Not only does smiling benefit you, but also those around you. Smiles are warm, contagious, and can light up a room. Use the power of your smile when you truly desire to improve your mood or to spread positive energy to those around you.

Smile Activity

This activity will help give you a boost of instant sunshine.

Find a mirror or open your phone's camera and smile at yourself like you would when greeting a close friend or lover.

Notice how this positively affected you. Do this anytime you need a healthy dose of positivity.

Vibe Higher: Set Intentions

Intentions, goals, dreams, wishes, whatever you'd like to call them, help you get clear on what it is you desire. They provide a framework to help you live your life on purpose. The act of writing or speaking your intentions gives them more power and can increase your vibration by up to 60%. The reason this increases your vibration is because scattered thoughts are low vibrating, whereas specific, clear-headed thoughts are higher vibrating.

When setting your intentions, write or record them as if it is already reality for you. For example, *I love living in my dream home with my beautiful family in California*. Avoid using these low-vibrating phrases in your intentions:

- *I hope...*
- *I will...*
- *I want...*
- *I need...*

You can replace these low-vibrating phrases with these higher vibrating options:

- *I am...*
- *I choose...*
- *I have...*
- *I love...*

Also be careful to avoid negative words in your intentions. It's popular for people to desire to be debt-free, but debt is very negative, even with a hyphenated free following it. Financial freedom is much higher vibrating and better supports the desired outcome. Financial freedom indicates the ability to give and receive as you wish. See how that is more powerful than *not having debt*?

Intentions can be set for both short-term and long-term and can be about any part of your life: family, finance, career, love and relationships, spirituality, you name it. It is helpful to choose your words carefully and be specific. Intentions can be set at any time, but the power behind your intentions can be multiplied when you create them during the new moon. New moon energy is perfect for planting the seeds of your desires. When setting intentions during a new moon, state and record them as you prefer and offer them to the new moon energy to help your intentions absorb the energy.

Intention Setting Exercise

Choose your medium: special pen/paper, computer, or smartphone. Think about what you truly desire in your life.

You can focus on one thing or anything that comes to mind. There is no limit. Get specific about what you would like your reality to be. Record your intentions on your paper or, if you prefer a digital approach, you can record a voice memo or type your note.

Tuck your intentions away and set a calendar reminder to review your intentions 90 days from now. When you look at your intentions, see what you've actualized, and which ones are in motion.

You are now aware of the many ways to raise and maintain your vibrations and have so many high vibing activities to add to your toolbelt. There are times you might feel you need extra energetic support. Let's keep moving and talk about caring for your energy with a helper.

Caring for Your Energy with a Helper

"Never let your ego get in the way of asking for help when in desperate need. We have all been helped at a point in our lives."
-Edmond Mbiaka

There are so many things we can do ourselves to care for our energy, but sometimes we do need help. Oftentimes the issues we are experiencing on the surface are deeply rooted energetic issues. Non-beneficial energy can get stuck and create blockages that lead to undesirable situations. Energy healers are holistic providers who identify and release non-beneficial energy affecting you. The clearing of non-beneficial energy is incredibly helpful to the mind, body, and spirit and necessary for optimal well-being.

There are many different types of holistic providers to help you care for your energy. Having an energy healer should be just as common as having an auto mechanic, a dentist, or a hairstylist. You care for your car, teeth, and hair regularly, but see your mechanic, dentist, or hairstylist periodically for a tune-up. Caring for your energy and scheduling regular "tune-ups" will help you maintain a healthy vibration.

It is possible some people may need to see a holistic healer more frequently in the beginning of their healing journey. If you've been experiencing issues for some time, be sure to allow for patience to realize your desired results if you are having holistic healing for the first time. It is also possible people may need to seek out more than one type of holistic healer. While the end goal for all healers is optimal wellness, love, and light, there are different methods to achieve these desired results. Let's explore different types of holistic providers who focus on caring for your energy:

Access Consciousness Providers clear consciousness and non-beneficial programming keeping people stuck in undesirable realities.

Acupuncturists utilize acupuncture needles to free stuck energy from energetic meridians in the body.

Angelic Liaisons/Spiritual Advisers communicate with archangels and other spiritual helpers and guides to assist you.

Aromatherapists use essential oils to clear non-beneficial energy and infuse with beneficial energy.

BodyTalk Practitioners follow a detailed protocol to identify and release non-beneficial energy for people and animals.

Emotional Freedom Technique Practitioners help individuals release non-beneficial energy, fears, thoughts, and beliefs through tapping and effective tapping language.

Pendulum Dowsers utilize a pendulum to identify issues and clear, measure, and shift energy for people, places, nature, animals, and objects in the past, present, and future.

Reflexologists work with the feet to identify and resolve issues within the body.

Reiki Practitioners use their hands with light or no touching to scan the body and identify and release non-beneficial energy for people and animals.

Sound Therapists use sound to clear and balance vibrations for people, animals, and places.

It can be overwhelming to decide which helper or service you need, or you might have limited access to holistic health providers in your community. Energy does not know space and time like we do, so many types of energy healing services are just as effective at a distance as they are face-to-face. Geography and time constraints should never create a barrier for anyone seeking energetic support. Most professionals will be able to identify what method of healing will be most beneficial for you and can even make referrals if other types of services are needed.

How to Tell if You Need a Holistic Healer

You might be wondering if you need support from an energy healer. Here are indicators that it is time to seek assistance from a helper:

- You are actively working to improve your current situation but are not seeing the results you desire.
- You feel drawn to a particular person or business offering holistic healing services.
- You have a family history of illness, disease, or misfortune that seems to span more than one generation.
- You have had a traumatic experience.

I like to refer to energy healing as a bath for the soul. People are often drawn to energy healing because it can provide clarity and resolve for issues they are experiencing. Many of my clients can physically feel the energy shifting during their appointments and immediately after report feeling lighter, like a weight lifted off their shoulders.

Holistic healers aren't the only helpers you can call on. Let me introduce you to other helpers and how to work with them in the next chapter.

Calling on Spiritual Helpers

"Make friends with the angels...and make
good use of their help and assistance in all
your temporal and spiritual affairs."
-Saint Francis de Sales

You have a whole spirit team that is just your own, and there are also spirit helpers you can call on to help you with something specific. Archangels, goddesses, ancestors, animals, and spirit guides are some examples. You can call on your spirit team or other spirit helpers anytime to support you. You don't have to wait for big issues to ask for their help; they are willing to assist you with anything.

Calling on spiritual helpers is similar to praying or meditating with a specific purpose in mind, only this time you are requesting support, feedback, or energy from a spiritual helper. Perhaps you would like guidance, clarity, or encouragement to help you move forward. You might just want the energy of the spirit helpers to lift you up. Maybe you would just like someone to talk to. You can talk to spirit any time you wish about anything you desire.

Some people are hesitant to ask for help. They worry they will seem greedy or that their issues aren't big enough or deserving of spiritual support. This is simply untrue. I previously had not realized that any and all worries could be offered to spirit. I remember when I first discovered I could pray for guidance in my business- what a revelation for me! We don't ever have to feel alone in our struggles or desires, because spirit is here to illuminate our path when we ask them to.

Your Spirit Team

Each of us has a spirit team that is just our own. Your spirit team was formed when you decided to have an earthly human experience. This team always has your back, and you can tap into their energy anytime you choose to. Spirit teams can grow after birth as helpers join to assist you with something specific going on in your life. As such, it is quite common that some members of your spirit team might no longer be helpful for your highest good later in life. This doesn't mean they are intentionally causing negativity in your life, but it can make it difficult for you to move along your path if they are no longer in alignment with you. Think of it like the old school employee who means well, but has difficulty accepting change. As you can imagine, this could affect the cohesiveness of your spirit team and directly impact you.

It is important to thank these team members for their

service and let them go. A holistic healer can assist you with this, or you can do this yourself by stating:

*Is there anyone on my spirit team no longer
supporting my highest good? If so, I thank you
for your service and now release you.*

If you are like me, you might initially feel conflicted about letting go a spirit being who was here to support you, but I assure you, it is OK because you are letting them go with love and kindness, and they are understanding.

Just as you can check in to see if any spirit guides are no longer serving your highest good, you can ask if there are any spirit helpers who would like to join your team by stating:

*Is there anyone serving my highest good who would
like to join my spirit team? I welcome you.*

Both releasing and adding spirit team members can be done every few months or when you feel necessary.

You can call on other spiritual helpers outside of your spirit team at any time. Spiritual helpers you can call on include Source, Jesus Christ, archangels, goddesses, spirit guides, animal spirit guides, and others. If you are unsure who to call on, just ask for any spiritual helpers willing to assist you that are beneficial to your highest good. At the end of this section, the Spirit Helper Exercise will guide you on how to do this.

Spirits

Call on spirits as you need them, invite them into your life, and thank them for their unconditional love. There are spirit helpers for almost everything. Here are examples of spirits you might choose to call upon to help raise your vibration:

- Spirit of Abundance
- Spirit of Animals
- Spirit of Appreciation
- Spirit of Authenticity
- Spirit of Balance
- Spirit of Christ
- Spirit of Communication
- Spirit of Discernment
- Spirit of Environment
- Spirit of Forgiveness
- Spirit of Freedom
- Spirit of Frequency
- Spirit of Gratitude
- Spirit of Healing
- Spirit of Hope
- Spirit of Imperfections
- Spirit of Karma
- Spirit of Land
- Spirit of Learning
- Spirit of Light
- Spirit of Love
- Spirit of Nature
- Spirit of Patience

- Spirit of Prosperity
- Spirit of Protection
- Spirit of Receiving
- Spirit of Relationships
- Spirit of Releasing
- Spirit of Spirits
- Spirit of Water
- Spirit of Wisdom
- Spirit of Wellness

Archangels

Archangels are incredibly powerful, well-known spiritual helpers. They are non-denominational and are willing to support anyone requesting their assistance. Each archangel has a specialty and energy for which they are responsible. Here are brief descriptions of the main energy type of each Archangel:

- Archangel Ariel – confident and wishful
- Archangel Azrael – sympathetic and empathetic
- Archangel Chamuel – love and guidance
- Archangel Gabriel – pure and creative
- Archangel Haniel – realistic and passionate
- Archangel Jeremiel – imaginative and courageous
- Archangel Jophiel – wise and beautiful
- Archangel Metatron – compassionate and playful
- Archangel Michael – protective and courageous
- Archangel Raguel – intelligent and whimsical
- Archangel Raphael – healing and nurturing
- Archangel Raziel – sentimental and faithful

- Archangel Sandalphon – tolerant and daring
- Archangel Uriel – peaceful and comforting
- Archangel Zadkiel – freedom and forgiveness

Divine Feminine Ascended Masters

You may feel drawn to the spirits of Divine Feminine Ascended Masters. Re-introduced to our consciousness by Kaia Ra, author of *The Sophia Code*, these spiritual beings are willing to assist you when called upon. Here are summaries of the main energies of these Ascended Masters:

- Green Tara – compassion and purity
- Hathor – feminine and cosmic renewal
- Isis – magic and rebirth
- Mary Magdalene – strength and transformation
- Mother Mary – unconditional love and mind, body, spirit alignment
- Quan Yin – mercy and compassion
- White Buffalo Woman – karma and authenticity

You might find yourself favoring certain spirit guides and spiritual helpers more so than others. That is completely normal. It is quite possible you have a deeper spiritual connection with them at this moment in time or for all the time. I have been told numerous times the energy of Archangel Jophiel is with me. When I first heard this, I was an archangel rookie and eager to learn more. I consciously made an effort to communicate with her and incorporate her presence into my life. I know people who communicate with one or two spirit guides more frequently than their other spirit guides. Building relationships with spiritual guides and helpers is not unlike building relationships with people, except spiritual beings always love you unconditionally and place no judgement on you.

How to Call on Spirit

To call on a spiritual helper, simply state:

> *<<INSERT SPIRIT HELPER NAME>>, please fill me with your pure divine and loving energy. Thank you. Thank you. Thank you.*

Calling on Spirit When You Have an Issue

To call on a spiritual helper, say:

> *<<INSERT SPIRIT HELPER NAME>>, please assist me with overcoming <<INSERT ISSUE>> so I may experience <<INSERT DESIRE>> as I truly desire. Thank you. Thank you. Thank you.*

Allow yourself to embrace the energy of your spirit helper. Be especially conscious of spirit trying to communicate with you over the next several days through signs, symbols, messages, and the feeling of a warm and loving presence.

Vibing High, but Experiencing Challenges

"Challenges make you discover things about
yourself that you never really knew."
-Cicely Tyson

It is possible to experience challenges even at your ideal frequency. When I say challenges, I mean things that annoy you, irritate you, stress you, etc. Challenges can be experienced physically, emotionally, and spiritually. They are an alert that it's time to make a change, or "level up" as my good friend The Salty Spiritualist says. Challenges are a time to learn something new, experience growth, increase your awareness, or make a change. Why would you make a change when things are going really great? Chances are you wouldn't, so a challenge can be a spiritual nudge to keep you moving along your path.

Sometimes the challenge itself is obvious to what needs

your attention. Maybe an item you've been hanging onto for too long goes missing or breaks. Maybe you are let go from a job where you felt miserable. On the other hand, sometimes challenges can be difficult to understand.

Anything you are experiencing right now that you consider challenging could have a spiritual meaning attached to it. What does it mean spiritually when my windshield cracks? What does it mean spiritually when my washing machine quits working? What is the spiritual meaning of backaches? The Internet is an incredible resource for deciphering spiritual meanings. Look up your challenge to see if there is a spiritual meaning that resonates with you.

Challenges usually persist until they are addressed. Challenges aren't always fun or pretty, but you can find comfort in knowing that if you are willing to do the work, learn the lesson, and grow from the experience, you will come out of the situation stronger, wiser, and with greater abilities. If you have difficulty sorting through your challenges on your own, seek assistance from a holistic healer or spiritual helper for guidance.

You might notice spiritual helpers trying to communicate with you as well. Seeing numbers, animals, or objects frequently or in odd places could indicate a very important message for you. A person saying something that seems random yet completely resonates with you could be spiritual helpers using someone else to communicate to you. And if you're really lucky, you might actually hear the messages, either aurally or just by knowing as if you've always known it. When you're paying attention and working closely with your spirit helpers, you will see special messages all around you. If you are uncertain what spirit is trying to communicate with you, ask for more clarity or meditate and pray on it.

Knowing Your Vibes

"The closer you come to knowing that you alone create
the world of your experience, the more vital it becomes
for you to discover just who is doing the creating."
-Eric Micha'el Leventhal

Can we just take a minute to talk about how amazing you
are? You just took time for yourself to learn about energy,
frequency, and how to vibe higher. All of this to help you feel
and do your best and to be the brightest light you can be in
this world! Reflect on your experience:

What have you learned about yourself?

Have you discovered what you are like when you vibe
high?

What are you like when you're vibing low?

Which ways do you like best for caring for your energy?

Be proud of yourself. You are a high vibin' machine! Anytime you feel your frequency dropping or you need an energetic boost, go back to the Vibe Higher exercises, call on a helper, and take care of you. You are well on your way to loving life like you were meant to and experiencing all that you truly desire. You, my friend, are awesome.

"Help me to believe the truth about myself,
no matter how beautiful it may be."
-Steve Chandler

Additional Resources

Thank you so much for checking out Vibe Higher. Learn more about Serena James at www.authorserenajames.com.

Connect with Serena James on social media:

- Facebook www.facebook.com/authorserenajames
- Instagram @authorserenajames
- Twitter @AuthorSerena

Continue to explore the power of energy at Serena James' holistic healing headquarters, Just Be, at www. thejustbelifestyle.com. You will find:

- Energy healing services
- Articles about energy and healthy living
- Upcoming events and workshops
- Natural wellness products and more

Connect with Just Be on social media:

- Facebook www.facebook.com/thejustbelifestyle
- Instagram @thejustbelifestyle
- Pinterest https://www.pinterest.com/thejustbelifestyle
- Twitter @justbelifestyle

Acknowledgements

My publishing team who guided me through this process from start to finish and beyond, thank you for keeping me on track.

Thank you to my family and friends for the love and encouragement to embrace my calling as a lightworker and supporting me every step along the way.

My friend The Salty Spiritualist, Sarah Jacobs, for reviewing the very first version *Vibe Higher* and providing valuable feedback to make it even better.

My parents and sister for allowing me to believe I can do anything and always being my sounding board for my wild ideas.

My loving partner for his unending encouragement and his willingness to read through multiple drafts of *Vibe Higher* to find my errors.

And my son for believing one million percent I can bring holistic healing to the forefront of people's minds and actions all over the world. You are my why. I love you.

I am forever grateful.

Be love. Be light. Just Be.

Helpful Terms and Definitions

Affirmation: intentional statements (recited, read or listened to) to encourage positive change and personal growth.

Aromatherapy: the use of essential oils to benefit the mind, body, and spirit.

Aura: the energetic field surrounding all living beings.

Chakras: energy centers in the body but can also exist in physical structures and nature.

Desire: a higher vibrating replacement for the word *want*.

Empath: a person who has the natural ability to tap into Universal energy and, when aware, can transmute that energy to something more beneficial.

Energetic Filter: an unseen field of energy put into place around a person or place with the intention of providing protection from non-beneficial energy.

Energy: the life force that exists within and outside of everything.

Energy Healer: a type of holistic healer focused on appropriately shifting, releasing, and infusing energy for people, places, nature, animals, and objects for optimal well-being.

Frequency: how energy is measured.

Holistic Healer: a person who provides solutions and support of the whole person focusing on the mind, body, and spirit.

Ideal Frequency: the frequency at which all things function at their best.

Law of Attraction: a widely accepted concept of you get what you give, think about, and believe.

Pendulum: a hand-held energy healing tool used in dowsing, usually a weighted object at the end of a string or chain.

Pendulum Dowsing: the practice of utilizing a pendulum to measure, shift, release, and infuse energy.

About the Author

Serena James is a certified holistic healer tasked with the exciting life mission of raising the vibration of Mother Earth. She provides energy healing services and workshops to help people overcome energetic barriers to experience more joy, wellness, and abundance in their lives. James is the founder of Just Be and makes her home in the beautiful state of Montana with her family. Please visit www.thejustbelifestyle. com for further information.

Printed in the United States
By Bookmasters